THE RISING TERRORIST THREAT AND THE UNFULFILLED 9/11 RECOMMENDATION

HEARING

BEFORE THE

COMMITTEE ON HOMELAND SECURITY
HOUSE OF REPRESENTATIVES

ONE HUNDRED THIRTEENTH CONGRESS

SECOND SESSION

JULY 23, 2014

Serial No. 113–79

Printed for the use of the Committee on Homeland Security

Available via the World Wide Web: http://www.gpo.gov/fdsys/

U.S. GOVERNMENT PRINTING OFFICE

91–931 PDF   WASHINGTON : 2015

For sale by the Superintendent of Documents, U.S. Government Printing Office
Internet: bookstore.gpo.gov   Phone: toll free (866) 512–1800; DC area (202) 512–1800
Fax: (202) 512–2250   Mail: Stop SSOP, Washington, DC 20402–0001

COMMITTEE ON HOMELAND SECURITY

MICHAEL T. McCAUL, Texas, *Chairman*

LAMAR SMITH, Texas
PETER T. KING, New York
MIKE ROGERS, Alabama
PAUL C. BROUN, Georgia
CANDICE S. MILLER, Michigan, *Vice Chair*
PATRICK MEEHAN, Pennsylvania
JEFF DUNCAN, South Carolina
TOM MARINO, Pennsylvania
JASON CHAFFETZ, Utah
STEVEN M. PALAZZO, Mississippi
LOU BARLETTA, Pennsylvania
RICHARD HUDSON, North Carolina
STEVE DAINES, Montana
SUSAN W. BROOKS, Indiana
SCOTT PERRY, Pennsylvania
MARK SANFORD, South Carolina
CURTIS CLAWSON, Florida

BENNIE G. THOMPSON, Mississippi
LORETTA SANCHEZ, California
SHEILA JACKSON LEE, Texas
YVETTE D. CLARKE, New York
BRIAN HIGGINS, New York
CEDRIC L. RICHMOND, Louisiana
WILLIAM R. KEATING, Massachusetts
RON BARBER, Arizona
DONDALD M. PAYNE, JR., New Jersey
BETO O'ROURKE, Texas
FILEMON VELA, Texas
ERIC SWALWELL, California
VACANCY
VACANCY

BRENDAN P. SHIELDS, *Staff Director*
JOAN O'HARA, *Acting Chief Counsel*
MICHAEL S. TWINCHEK, *Chief Clerk*
I. LANIER AVANT, *Minority Staff Director*

(II)

CONTENTS

THE RISING TERRORIST THREAT AND THE UNFULFILLED 9/11 RECOMMENDATION

Wednesday, July 23, 2014

U.S. HOUSE OF REPRESENTATIVES,
COMMITTEE ON HOMELAND SECURITY,
Washington, DC.

The committee met, pursuant to call, at 10:11 a.m., in Room 311, Cannon House Office Building, Hon. Michael T. McCaul [Chairman of the committee] presiding.

Present: Representatives McCaul, King, Rogers, Broun, Meehan, Marino, Palazzo, Barletta, Daines, Brooks, Thompson, Jackson Lee, Clarke, Barber, Payne, O'Rourke, and Vela.

Chairman McCAUL. The Committee on Homeland Security will come to order. The committee is meeting today to examine key issues contained in the Bipartisan Policy Center's research report marking the 10th anniversary of the release of the original 9/11 Commission report. I now recognize myself for an opening statement.

Ten years after the 9/11 Commission provided recommendations to prevent other terrorist attacks on the United States soil, the terror threat from abroad remains real, and we will continue to be challenged identifying home-grown terrorists.

The current instability in the Middle East, the web of al-Qaeda affiliates, and the rapid advance of extremist ISIS militants are fueling the rise of new safe havens where terrorists live, train, and plot future attacks.

In a recently-released anniversary report, the former members of the commission reflect on the progress made and provide recommendations on how to further enhance the security of the United States. Specifically, the new report concludes that some recommendations from the commission remain unfulfilled, and one in particular has been largely ignored: Reforming Congressional jurisdiction over the Department of Homeland Security.

In 2004, the 9/11 Commission recognized the importance of eliminating terrorist safe havens. The report stated, "Terrorists should no longer find safe havens where their organizations can grow and flourish. Our efforts should be accompanied by a preventative strategy that is as much, or more, political as is military."

Those words were written a decade ago, yet safe havens for terrorists not only still exist, they have expanded and beyond the regions where the 9/11 attacks originated.

For instance, ISIS, an organization too extreme for al-Qaeda, has made alarming territorial gains in both Syria and Iraq, establishing the largest terrorist safe haven since 9/11. The group's leader, al-Baghdadi, has declared himself head of a new Muslim caliphate. ISIS has the ambition and now the funding, weapons, and manpower to launch attacks against United States' interests abroad and possibly into the homeland.

Furthermore, foreign fighters with valid travel documents are flooding into the region, many from Western countries, including the United States. Like ISIS, al-Nusra, the Syrian al-Qaeda affiliate, has established training camps catering not only to local extremists, but fighters coming from abroad. These camps serve as training grounds for many, including the American teenager from Florida who is believed to have carried out a suicide bomb attack in May. Although he carried out his attack in Syria, he could have instead attempted to travel back into the United States following his training.

Self-radicalized terrorists like Nidal Hassan, who fatally shot 13 people at Fort Hood in 2009, and Tamerlan Tsarnaev, one of the perpetrators of the Boston Marathon bombings, were allegedly influenced or used such extremist propaganda, rich with content from jihadi fighting. The threats to the homeland extend beyond the traditional battlefield also into the cyber realm.

American companies, universities, defense capabilities, and critical infrastructure are all under cyber attack. Most concerning, however, is that the threat is outpacing our readiness to combat it. One expert described our cyber preparedness as being at "September 10 levels." My concern is that history will repeat itself when it comes to cyber and we will not, as a Nation, acknowledge the gravity of the threat until it is too late.

Another unfulfilled commission recommendation also threatens American security. The continued fragmentation of Congressional oversight of the Department of Homeland Security makes us less agile in the face of these growing threats. DHS is forced to expend scarce resources reporting to far too many Congressional committees, resources that could be spent protecting the American people. Ironically, this excess of oversight actually leads to a lack of accountability because of the mixed signals and conflicting demands of Congressional committees.

In fiscal year 2013, according to the Department of Homeland Security, the agency facilitated more than 1,650 briefings with Members of Congress or their staff, provided 161 witnesses who testified at 105 hearings, and engaged with nearly all Members of Congress and dozens, if not 100 committees. This cost taxpayers tens of millions of dollars and cost DHS 66 work years in man-hours.

To address these flaws, the 9/11 Commission Report recommended that Congress "create a single, principal point of oversight and review for homeland security." This critical step has yet to be taken, and it is cited in the commission's latest report.

Just as the National Security Act of 1947 reorganized the United States Government's military and intelligence agencies into a unified Federal structure, the Homeland Security Act of 2002 unified several agencies into a single organization to coordinate and unify National homeland security efforts. While these changes were accepted by the administration, Congress, in many cases, is still working under pre-9/11 authorities.

Congress needs to create clear jurisdictional lines to ensure that DHS receives strong, centralized oversight and can focus its efforts on its mission to protect the United States. These steps are necessary to ensure the safety and security of the homeland.

In the mean time, my committee will spend significant time the remainder of this year and in the next Congress authorizing key DHS components. Moreover, in partnership with the other committees of jurisdiction, I intend to lead the first-ever DHS authorization through regular order.

We are fortunate today to have the chairman of the 9/11 Commission, along with the former commissioner, Jamie Gorelick, here today to offer their insights and perspectives. I hope our hearing will help us create actionable solutions that can address these shortcomings sooner rather than later.

I would like the opportunity today to thank the 9/11 victims' families who are with us here today. Through their persistent efforts, the 9/11 Commission was established to investigate that horrific attack on U.S. soil that we will always remember and never forget. We thank them for their continued commitment to secure the homeland.

[The statement of Chairman McCaul follows:]

STATEMENT OF CHAIRMAN MICHAEL T. MCCAUL

JULY 23, 2014

Ten years after the 9/11 Commission provided recommendations to prevent other terrorist attacks on United States soil the terror threat from abroad remains real, and we will continue to be challenged in identifying home-grown terrorists. The current instability in the Middle East, the web of al-Qaeda affiliates and the rapid advance of extremist ISIS militants are fueling the rise of new safe havens where terrorists live, train, and plot future attacks.

In a recently-released anniversary report, the former members of the Commission reflect on the progress made and provide recommendations on how to further enhance the security of the United States. Specifically, the new report concludes that some recommendations from the Commission remain unfulfilled and one in particular has been largely ignored—reforming Congressional jurisdiction over the Department of Homeland Security.

In 2004, the 9/11 Commission recognized the importance of eliminating terrorist safe havens. The report stated: "Terrorists should no longer find safe haven where their organizations can grow and flourish . . . Our efforts should be accompanied by a preventative strategy that is as much, or more, political as it is military." Those words were written a decade ago—yet safe havens for terrorists not only still exist, they have expanded well beyond the regions where the 9/11 attacks originated.

For instance, ISIS—an organization too extreme for al-Qaeda—has made alarming territorial gains in both Syria and Iraq, establishing the largest terrorist safe haven since 9/11. The group's leader, Abu Bakr al-Baghdadi, has declared himself head of a new Muslim caliphate. ISIS has the ambition and now the funding, weapons, and manpower to launch attacks against U.S. interests abroad and possibly the homeland.

Furthermore, foreign fighters with valid travel documents are flooding into the region; many from Western countries including the United States. Like ISIS, al-Nusra, the Syrian al-Qaeda affiliate, has established training camps catering not only to local extremists but fighters coming from abroad. These camps served as training grounds for many including the American teenager from Florida who is believed to have carried out a suicide bomb attack in May. Although he carried out his attack in Syria, Abusahla could have instead attempted to travel back to the United States following his training.

Self-radicalized terrorists like Nidal Hassan, who fatally shot 13 people at Fort Hood in 2009, and Tamerlan Tsarnaev, one of the perpetrators of the Boston Marathon bombings, were allegedly influenced or used such extremist propaganda, rich with content from jihadi fighting.

The threats to the homeland extend beyond the traditional battlefield into the cyber realm. American companies, universities, defense capabilities, and critical infrastructure are all under cyber attack. Most concerning, however, is that the threat is outpacing our readiness to combat it. One expert described our cyber-preparedness as being at "September 10 levels." My concern is that history will repeat itself when it comes to cyber and we will not, as a Nation, acknowledge the gravity of the threat until it is too late.

Another unfulfilled Commission recommendation also threatens American security. The continued fragmentation of Congressional oversight of the Department of Homeland Security makes us less agile in the face of these growing threats. DHS is forced to expend scarce resources reporting to far too many Congressional committees—resources that could be spent protecting the American people.

Ironically, this excess of oversight actually leads to a lack of accountability because of the mixed signals and conflicting demands of Congressional committees. In fiscal year 2013, according to the Department of Homeland Security, the agency facilitated more than 1,650 briefings with Members of Congress or their staff, provided 161 witnesses who testified at 105 hearings, and engaged with nearly all Members of Congress and dozens of committees. This cost taxpayers tens of millions of dollars and cost DHS 66 work years in man-hours.

To address these flaws, 9/11 Commission Report recommended that Congress "create a single, principal point of oversight and review for homeland security." This critical step has yet to be taken and is cited in the Commission's latest report.

Just as the National Security Act of 1947 reorganized the United States Government's military and intelligence agencies into a unified Federal structure, the Homeland Security Act of 2002 unified several agencies into a single organization to coordinate and unify National homeland security efforts. While these changes were accepted by the administration, Congress, in many cases, is still working under pre-9/11 authorities.

Congress needs to create clear jurisdictional lines to ensure that DHS receives strong, centralized oversight and can focus its efforts on its mission to protect the United States. These steps are necessary to ensure the safety and security of the homeland.

In the meantime, my committee will spend significant time the remainder of this year and into the next Congress authorizing key DHS components. Moreover in partnership with the other committees of jurisdiction, I intend to lead the first ever DHS authorization through regular order.

We are fortunate today to have the co-chair of the 9/11 Commission Tom Kean, as well as former Commissioner Jamie Gorelick here to offer their insights and perspectives. I hope our hearing will help us create actionable solutions that can address these shortcomings sooner rather than later.

I would like to take this opportunity to recognize the 9/11 victims' families who are with us today. Through their persistent efforts, the 9/11 Commission was established to investigate that horrific attack on U.S. soil. We thank them for their continued commitment to secure the homeland.

Chairman MCCAUL. With that, the Chairman now recognizes the Ranking Member, Mr. Thompson.

Mr. THOMPSON. Thank you very much, Mr. Chairman. I thank you for holding today's hearing. I would also like to thank the witnesses for their testimony.

Ten years ago, the National Commission on Terrorist Attacks in the United States issued the official account of the terrorist attacks that occurred on September 11, 2001. In that report, the 9/11 Commission made a series of recommendations to strengthen our counterterrorism efforts, foster information sharing beyond traditional boundaries, and strengthen Congressional oversight to improve the effectiveness of homeland security measures.

While the Implementing 9/11 Commission Recommendations Act addressed many of these recommendations, challenges still remain. From the outset, the 9/11 Commission was tasked to make recommendations to prevent another terrorist attack. In the 10 years since the report's release, we have seen the terrorist threat change. The top leadership of al-Qaeda, the group that claimed responsibility for the 9/11 attacks, has been dismantled by the Obama administration.

Although al-Qaeda has been weakened, we remain vigilant about persistent and emerging threats. We must closely monitor the capabilities of al-Qaeda's affiliates who are thriving in the untenable areas such as Iraq and Syria. Though many of these groups' aspirations are localized to the countries in which they operate, they do not espouse anti-American views that are concerning.

We also must turn a blind eye to the threat of lone-wolf actors in the United States. Some of these people are inspired by al-Qaeda and domestic anti-Government and hate groups. From counterterrorism efforts to succeed, we need to do a better job of sharing information. That is the message from the 9/11 commissioners a decade ago, and that is their message today.

Last year's Boston Marathon bombing re-emphasized the need for improvements in information sharing between both Federal agencies and State and local authorities. The continued evolution and escalation of al-Qaeda and its affiliates abroad also underscores the need for strong intelligence and information partnerships with our foreign allies. I fear that some of our key relationships have been tested by high-profile leaks about NSA programs and other counterterrorism efforts. More needs to be done to fortify key information-sharing relationships.

Also, I appreciate that the Bipartisan Policy Committee has highlighted cybersecurity as an area of concern. As we become more dependent on technology, opportunities for cyberterrorism increase rapidly. Today, hostile nations, criminal groups, and individuals seek to exploit information networks to further a variety of individual, National, and ideological objectives. I have been a major proponent of DHS's efforts to foster cyber hygiene and timely information sharing, particularly among critical infrastructure's owners and operators.

Though I know it is directly related to today's proceedings, I do want to express, on the record, my hope that bipartisan cybersecurity legislation that was approved by the committee, Mr. Chairman, in February will be considered by the House hopefully before August. We need to do more to create an environment of vigilance that gives Americans confidence that their personal data is private and secure, and allow the Government to ensure the integrity of its information while identifying and prosecuting cyber criminals when possible.

Further, as the Bipartisan Policy Committee also notes in its report, the House, under both Democratic and Republican majorities, has failed to consolidate authorizing and oversight jurisdiction for each component of the Department of Homeland Security into one Congressional committee. I agree with the 9/11 commissioners that the fragmented oversight detracts from the Department's National security mission. We have seen it time and time again.

I am sure the Chairman would agree that this committee should be the authorizing and oversight committee of the Department of Homeland Security, but that comes with a price. The price is asserting jurisdiction. I have been in the Chairman's seat, tried to do it, and I welcome you to try to get it done under your leadership.

It is disappointing that with 8 voting weeks left in Congress, this committee is on track to receive its lowest number of referrals since its inception. Looking forward, as we continue to strengthen the Department of Homeland Security, we must not forget the terrorist threat, but recognize it is evolving.

Information sharing must be strengthened, and we must foster greater cybersecurity protections, particularly on the networks that are the backbone for critical infrastructure. I look forward to working in a bipartisan manner to fulfill these 9/11 recommendations.

With that, Mr. Chairman, I yield back the balance of my time.

[The statement of Ranking Member Thompson follows:]

STATEMENT OF RANKING MEMBER BENNIE G. THOMPSON

JULY 23, 2014

Ten years ago, the "National Commission on Terrorist Attacks in the United States" issued the official account of the terrorist attacks that occurred on September 11, 2001. In that report, the 9/11 Commission made a series of recommendations to strengthen our counterterrorism efforts, foster information sharing beyond traditional boundaries, and strengthen Congressional oversight to improve the effectiveness of homeland security measures.

While the "Implementing 9/11 Commission Recommendations Act" addressed many of these recommendations, challenges still remain. From the outset, the 9/11 Commission was tasked to make recommendations to prevent another terrorist attack. In the 10 years since the report's release, we have seen the terrorist threat change. The top leadership for al-Qaeda, the group that claimed responsibility for the 9/11 attacks, has been dismantled by the Obama administration. Although al-Qaeda has been weakened exponentially, we remain vigilant about persistent and emerging threats. We must closely monitor the capabilities of al-Qaeda's affiliates who are thriving in unstable areas such as Iraq and Syria. Though many of these groups' aspirations are localized to the countries in which they operate, they do espouse anti-American views that are concerning.

We also must not turn a blind eye to the threat of lone wolf actors in the United States. Some of these people are inspired by al-Qaeda and domestic anti-Government and hate groups. For counterterrorism efforts to succeed, we need to do a better job of sharing information. That is the message from the 9/11 commissioners a decade ago and that is their message today. Last year's Boston Marathon Bombing reemphasized the need for improvements in information sharing between both Federal agencies and State and local authorities.

The continued evolution and escalation of al-Qaeda and its affiliates abroad also underscores the need for strong intelligence and information partnerships with our foreign allies. I fear that some of our key relationships have been tested by high-profile leaks about NSA programs and other counterterrorism efforts. More needs to be done to fortify key information-sharing relationships.

Also, I appreciate that the Bipartisan Policy Committee has highlighted cybersecurity as an area of concern. As we become more dependent on technology, opportunities for cyberterrorism increase rapidly. Today, hostile nations, criminal groups, and individuals seek to exploit information networks to further a variety of individual, National, and ideological objectives. I have been a major proponent of DHS's efforts to foster cyber hygiene and timely information sharing, particularly among critical infrastructure owners and operators.

Though I know it is directly related to today's proceedings, I do want to express, on the record, my hope that bipartisan cybersecurity legislation that was approved by the committee in February will be considered by the House before August. We need to do more to create an environment of vigilance that gives Americans confidence that their personal data is private and secure, and allow the Government to ensure the integrity of its information while identifying and prosecuting cyber criminals when possible.

Further, as the Bipartisan Policy Committee also notes in its report, the House, under both Democratic and Republican majorities, has failed to consolidate authorizing and oversight jurisdiction for each component of the Department of Homeland Security into one Congressional committee. I agree with the 9/11 Commissioners that the fragmented oversight detracts from the Department's National security mission. We have seen it time and again.

I am sure the Chairman would agree that this committee should be the authorizing and oversight committee of the Department of Homeland Security, but that comes with a price. That price is asserting jurisdiction. It is disappointing that with 8 voting weeks left this Congress, this committee is on track to receive its lowest number of referrals since its inception. Looking forward, as we continue to strengthen the Department of Homeland Security, we must not forget the terrorist threat, but recognize it is evolving.

Information sharing must be strengthened and we must foster greater cybersecurity protections, particularly on the networks that are the backbone for critical infrastructure. I look forward to working in a bipartisan manner to fulfill these 9/11 recommendations.

Chairman McCAUL. Thank the Ranking Member. I would like to enter into the record reflections on the 10th anniversary of the 9/11 Commission Report that just came out, and great work on the part of the commission. Without objection, so ordered.*

We are honored today to have two distinguished witnesses, members of the 9/11 Commission. First, the Honorable Thomas Kean is the co-chair of the Homeland Security Project at the Bipartisan Policy Center. We had a great discussion there yesterday, and I thank the two of you for that.

He is also the former chairman of the National Commission on Terrorist Attacks Upon the United States. The 9/11 Commission released its report in 2004, which has been an integral part in shaping American National security. Prior to chairing the 9/11 Commission, he served as Governor of New Jersey and president of Drew University.

Sir, thank you for being here.

Next, we have the Honorable Jamie Gorelick. As a former commissioner on the National Commission on Terrorist Attacks Upon the United States, currently she is a partner at WilmerHale, where she chairs the defense, National security, and Government contracts practice group. She was one of the longest-serving deputy attorneys general of the United States, under which I was proud to serve as a low-level line Federal prosecutor in the public integrity section. Prior to joining—I don't know if she remembers me or not, but I certainly remember her. Prior to joining the Department of Justice, Ms. Gorelick served as the general counsel for the Department of Defense.

We thank both of you for being here. I now recognize Governor Kean for his testimony.

STATEMENT OF THOMAS H. KEAN, JR., CO-CHAIR, HOMELAND SECURITY PROJECT, BIPARTISAN POLICY CENTER AND FORMER CHAIR, NATIONAL COMMISSION ON TERRORIST ATTACKS UPON THE UNITED STATES

Mr. KEAN. Thank you. Well, thank you both for inviting us, and thank the committee. This committee has done a great deal already to keep our country safer, and we thank you for that very much.

My friend and co-chairman Lee Hamilton hoped to be here with us today, but he cannot be, unfortunately. He was unable to come. So my colleague and friend, former 9/11 Commissioner Jamie Gorelick, joins me in appearing before you today. We are here, of course, to mark, for us, the 10th anniversary of the 9/11 Committee

---

*The information has been retained in committee files and is available at *http://bipartisanpolicy.org/wp-content/uploads/sites/default/files/files/%20BPC%209-11%20Commission.pdf.*

report, a document which, with your help, led to major reforms in National security.

Last fall, we started among ourselves—many of us haven't seen each other in 7, 8, 9 years—to consider how we might observe the 10th anniversary of our report. What we decided was we wanted to say something at that time which would help the American public understand the terrorist threat we face today and how that terrorist threat has changed over the last 10 years.

We also wanted to look back on how our own work 10 years ago—and we think there are lessons to be learned in how we have—how five Republicans and five Democrats happened to reach bipartisan and unanimous agreement, especially because we share the view that responding to the terrorist threat, taking the important steps needed to protect the country, is a part of our National security which simply must have a bipartisan approach.

To better inform ourselves, we reached out to many of our country's foremost senior, current, and former National security officials with responsibility for counterterrorism. We included names of many of the officials in our report, and they generously shared their time and did it with candor and frankness. They answered all our questions with clarity. They ducked none of them. We came away with the experience and renewed admiration for the fact that this Government continues to have a number of dedicated public servants in the security area.

We held separate conversations, by the way, with each one of these leaders, and yet we were struck by the fact that across all of them, there was really a broad consensus and a fear of the problems that were confronting us today and a worry whether the American people really had a perception of how the threat has changed and how serious that threat is today.

What we hope to succeed in doing in our paper is to amplify for the public these common threads that these security officials shared with us. I would like now to ask former Commissioner Jamie Gorelick to summarize what we learned and the key points in the paper.

[The joint prepared statement of Mr. Kean and Ms. Gorelick follows:]

JOINT PREPARED STATEMENT OF THOMAS H. KEAN, JR. AND JAMIE S. GORELICK

JULY 23, 2014

INTRODUCTION

Mr. Chairman, Mr. Ranking Member, Members of the committee: We are grateful for the opportunity to appear before you today. This committee has been at the center of improving our country's defenses against terrorist attacks. We are deeply grateful to you for your sustained support of the 9/11 Commission's recommendations and your leadership in reforming our National security institutions. Overseeing and guiding the Department of Homeland Security, which is still a young and evolving department, is one of the most important National security duties of the Congress. Over the past decade, this committee has been a steadfast champion of needed reform.

Today, we are appearing in our capacity as former 9/11 Commissioners. Governor Kean and Congressman Hamilton, the chair and vice chair of the 9/11 Commission, now lead the Homeland Security Project at the Bipartisan Policy Center. Drawing on a strong roster of National security professionals, the Project's mission is to be a bipartisan voice on homeland- and National-security issues. It works as an independent group to monitor the implementation of the 9/11 Commission's recommendations and address other emerging threats to our Nation.

On July 22, 2004, we issued *The 9/11 Commission Report*, the official report of the devastating attacks of September 11, 2001. Ten years later, the ten former members of the Commission reconvened, under the auspices of the Bipartisan Policy Center, to take stock of the terrorist threat and the country's readiness to face it.

CONTINUING TERRORIST THREAT FROM AL-QAEDA AND ITS AFFILIATES

When we wrote our report 10 years ago, we were acutely mindful of the responsibility we bore to the American people—and the families of the victims—to provide the most complete account possible of the events leading up to that terrible day. We used what we learned from that awful history to make recommendations as to how to make America safer. Today, we are pleased that most of those recommendations have been enacted into law or adopted as policy.

A decade after releasing our report, we are struck by how dramatically the world has changed. In the United States, Federal, State, and local authorities have implemented major security reforms to protect the country. Overseas, the United States and allies went on the offensive against al-Qaeda and related terrorist organizations. Ten years ago, many feared that al-Qaeda would launch more catastrophic attacks on the United States. That has not happened. While home-grown terrorists struck Fort Hood and the Boston Marathon, with tragic results, and while major attempted attacks on aviation have been disrupted, no attack on a scale approaching that of 9/11 has taken place.

U.S. and allied efforts have badly hurt "core" al-Qaeda, the organization that attacked us on 9/11. Al-Qaeda's leadership has been seriously diminished, most notably by the killing of Usama bin Ladin. The blows the United States has dealt those who struck us on 9/11 are a credit to the ceaseless work of dedicated men and women in our military and in our intelligence services, who often serve their country without accolades or even public acknowledgement.

However, the threat from jihadist terrorism persists. While core al-Qaeda has been damaged in recent years, its affiliates and associated groups have dispersed throughout the greater Middle East. Al-Qaeda spinoffs—some small, some worryingly large—now have a presence in more theaters of operation than they did half a decade ago, operating today in at least 16 countries.

In *The 9/11 Commission Report*, we said that one of the key lessons of the 9/11 story was that there can be "no sanctuaries" for terrorist groups. Geographic sanctuaries (like pre-9/11 Afghanistan) enable terrorist groups to gather, indoctrinate and train recruits, and they offer breathing space in which to develop complex plots (like the 9/11 attacks). The Islamic State in Iraq and Syria ("ISIS") now controls vast swaths of territory in Iraq and Syria, creating a massive terrorist sanctuary. Afghanistan could revert to that condition once American troops depart at the end of 2014. The recent Taliban offensive in Helmand Province illustrates that danger.

Meanwhile, al-Qaeda in the Arabian Peninsula ("AQAP") remains interested in striking the United States. The Saudi-born Ibrahim al-Asiri, AQAP's chief bomb maker, devised the underwear bomb worn by Umar Farouk Abdulmuttalab. Al-Asiri remains at large and there are concerns that he is gaining experience in the concealment and miniaturization of bombs and manufacturing them from nonmetallic materials, making them far harder to detect.

More than 10,000 foreign fighters have flooded into Syria. Once there, these fighters have access to on-the-job training in military operations, fashioning improvised explosive devices, and using assault weapons. Many come from Western Europe, but more than 70 are believed to be from the United States. One of these Americans, a Florida man in his early 20s, recently blew himself up in a suicide attack in northern Syria, the first instance of an American suicide bomber there. American counterterrorism and homeland security officials and European allies are deeply concerned that hardened fighters from Syria may redirect their venom and battlefield experience toward the United States or their European countries of origin. In at least one instance, this appears already to have happened: The suspect in the deadly May 24 shooting attack on the Jewish Museum in Brussels had spent more than a year in Syria, where he is believed to have joined up with jihadist groups.

Federal Bureau of Investigation Director James Comey has described the situation in Syria as, in several respects, "an order of magnitude worse" than the terrorist training ground that existed in Afghanistan before 9/11. It is unclear whether the United States and its allies have sufficient resources in place to monitor foreign fighters' activities in Syria (and neighboring Iraq) and to track their travel back to their home countries.

The convulsions across the Muslim world, from the Sahel to Pakistan, create opportunities for extremist groups to work their will. Opportunities to exert power may, to some extent, keep terrorists focused on their home regions. According to the State Department, terrorist attacks rose 43 percent worldwide in 2013. These attacks killed 17,891 and wounded 32,577. The Department reports that the vast majority of these incidents were local or regional, not international, in focus.

It does not follow, however, that terrorist groups have relaxed their enmity toward the United States and its allies. The 2012 attack on U.S. facilities in Benghazi, Libya, resulted in the deaths of four Americans, including the American ambassador. In 2013, al-Shabaab attacked the Westgate mall in Nairobi, Kenya, murdering more than 60 innocent people. These are reminders that dedicated terrorists can successfully execute deadly attacks against targets associated with the United States and the West.

Some National security officials believe that the forces of Islamist extremism in the Middle East are stronger than in the last decade. Partly, this is a consequence of the Arab Spring and the power vacuums and ungoverned spaces that have sprung up in its wake. Partly, it is the result of America's inability or reluctance to exert power and influence in a number of places. Officials are also deeply concerned about the region's seemingly endless supply of disaffected young people vulnerable to being recruited as suicide bombers. We explained in *The 9/11 Commission Report* that the "United States finds itself caught up in a clash within a civilization," which "arises from particular conditions in the Muslim world." This clash has only intensified since then.

Our assessment is that the terrorist threat is evolving, not defeated. Al-Qaeda's various spinoffs are, at the moment, enmeshed in their own local conflicts, but hatred of the United States remains a common thread. While some of these groups are not capable of striking the U.S. homeland, they may seek to attack outposts of the U.S. presence overseas, including diplomatic posts, military bases, or softer targets such as American businesses in foreign countries.

Home-grown terrorism remains a serious concern as well. Purveyors of hatred spread their radical ideology over the internet, attempting to recruit new terrorists both abroad and in the United States. The risk is not only that new terrorist cells are being created; on-line propaganda can also influence "lone wolf" terrorists, who can be extremely difficult for authorities to spot. The support of the American Muslim community in opposing extremism, increased awareness by the public at large, and a massive law enforcement effort have made the United States a much harder target than it was on 9/11. But the tragedy of the Boston Marathon bombing is a reminder of how dangerous home-grown extremists can be, despite these advances.

In sum, the terrorist threat has evolved, but it is still very real and very dangerous. The absence of another 9/11-style attack does not mean the threat is gone: As 9/11 showed, a period of quiet can be shattered in a moment by a devastating attack. The pressing question is whether the United States is prepared to face the emergent threats of today—and those it is likely to face in the years to come.

UNFINISHED BUSINESS

The Intelligence Reform and Terrorism Prevention Act of 2004 ushered in the most significant restructuring of the intelligence community since 1947. Despite this progress, some recommendations from *The 9/11 Commission Report* remain unimplemented.

First and foremost is reform of Congress's committee structure for overseeing homeland security. Your committee is Congress's expert on DHS and should be preeminent in terms of overseeing and legislating for the Department. Our recommendation of 10 years ago remains urgent today: "Through not more than one authorizing committee . . . in each house, Congress should be able to ask the Secretary of Homeland Security whether he or she has the resources to provide reasonable security against major terrorist acts within the United States and to hold the Secretary accountable for the department's performance." Regrettably, an unwieldy hodgepodge of other committees still exercises residual oversight and legislative jurisdiction over DHS. In 2004, we remarked with astonishment and alarm that DHS reported to 88 committees and subcommittees of Congress. Incredibly, DHS reports that that number has since increased, to 92.

This is not an academic concern. In *The 9/11 Commission Report*, we said that Congress, as a whole, adjusted slowly to the rise of transnational terrorism as a threat to National security. In the years before September 11, terrorism seldom registered as important, and Congress did not reorganize itself after the end of the Cold War to address new threats. Splintered committee jurisdiction resulted in episodic and inadequate attention to terrorism and to the overarching strategies needed to combat terrorist organizations. Put simply, when everyone is responsible, no one is.

We knew that, of "all our recommendations, strengthening Congressional oversight may be among the most difficult." Unfortunately, we were right. While the Executive branch has, at Congress's behest and urging, undergone historic change and institutional reform, Congress has proved deeply resistant to reforming its own structures for DHS oversight. In particular, it has delayed in yielding to this committee preeminent authorizing jurisdiction and oversight responsibility over all DHS components.

Again and again, past and present DHS senior managers have told us that this fragmented Congressional oversight is counterproductive to National security goals. DHS is still a young department, continually learning and striving to improve. Congress should help guide senior officials in managing the Department as a cohesive whole, rather than as a collection of disparate parts. The proliferation of oversight committees has the opposite effect. More than 90 different committees and subcommittees cannot develop expertise about the Department as a whole. Nor can committees that only oversee certain DHS components understand the effect of what they do on the Department's overall mission, or compare all of the competing priorities among which Department leaders must choose. Emblematic of this inability is the fact that Congress has not, since the Department's creation, enacted a final comprehensive DHS authorization bill setting policy and spending priorities for the Department.

Reporting to this vast array of committees also places an extraordinary administrative burden on DHS, which must prepare reams of written testimony and respond to countless questions for the record. This burden distracts from other, higher-priority tasks.

Effective Congressional oversight is especially important in areas, like homeland security, where much of the Government's activity necessarily occurs out of public view. Unlike other areas of policy, where the press and public can themselves monitor what their Government is doing, the public must rely on Congress to be its eyes and ears with respect to sensitive and Classified National security programs.

We have full confidence that this committee, and the Senate Committee on Homeland Security and Governmental Affairs, have the expertise and focus to best do that job for the American people. It is long past time for other committees to step back and allow you to fully take the reins for DHS. At the very minimum, the next Congress should sharply reduce the number of committees and subcommittees with some jurisdiction over the Department. The Department of Homeland Security should receive the same streamlined oversight as the Department of Defense.

These changes should take effect when the next Congress convenes and the House and Senate adopt new rules in January. Planning should begin now to make this possible.

The 9/11 Commission recommended creating a Director of National Intelligence (DNI) to oversee National intelligence centers on specific subjects of interest across the U.S. Government, and to manage the National intelligence program and oversee the agencies that contribute to it.

Congress created that office in the Intelligence Reform and Terrorism Prevention Act of 2004. Despite differences of view 10 years ago, senior leaders in the intelligence community today believe that the Office of the DNI has found its role in the National security apparatus. The DNI has been accepted as the manager of the community. Joint duty is becoming more common: More than 10,000 intelligence community civilian employees are certified as having done joint duty, with 1,000 doing so each year.

Many senior officials told us that personal chemistry among the leaders of the intelligence community and Pentagon is as important, if not more important, than legislated authority for the overall smooth and effective functioning of the National security system. It is not just a law that makes an organization or system work—it is the people. The current DNI's conception of his office has enabled him to successfully manage the community and elicit cooperation from its components. In particular, future DNIs should follow these key policies: (1) Coordinating the work of the various intelligence agencies, rather than replicating that work or turning ODNI itself into an operational entity; (2) advancing interagency information sharing, unified IT capabilities, joint duty, and other community-wide initiatives; and (3) providing centralized budgetary planning to ensure that the community as a whole possesses the most effective combination of tools.

Today, the Office of the DNI continues to be hampered by Congress's failure to update its practices to reflect post-9/11 reforms. One such anachronism: Intelligence community funds are not conveyed in a single appropriation. Instead, many community funds are buried in appropriations for the Department of Defense (DOD), a vestige of by-gone days when the top-line intelligence budget was Classified. With that figure now a matter of public record, there is no longer any reason to hide intelligence funds in the DOD budget.

A unified intelligence community budget, managed by the Director of National Intelligence and overseen by a single subcommittee in each house of Congress, would enable the DNI to manage community resources without navigating a bureaucratic labyrinth. It would also help ensure better oversight of the intelligence budget. Cohesive and comprehensive oversight of all intelligence community funding would be easier if appropriations for all 16 member agencies, plus ODNI, were conveyed in a single bill.

We believe that there is today greater agreement on this point than 10 years ago. We were particularly struck by the statement of a former senior leader of the Department of Defense that the DNI should have full authority to manage the intelligence community's budget. To that end, we reiterate our original recommendations: Congress should pass a separate appropriations act for the National Intelligence Program. The DNI should receive all funds appropriated in that bill and have full authority to apportion them among community agencies and reprogram them as needed to meet new priorities.

THE IMPORTANCE OF DATA COLLECTION AND ANALYSIS

In *The 9/11 Commission Report*, we noted the importance of intelligence collection and analysis in counterterrorism, and we recommended reforms to improve both. Intelligence gathering is the single most effective way to thwart terrorism—but identifying and finding terrorists, who go to great lengths to cover their tracks, is a very difficult task. Often no single report is definitive. Rather, it is the accumulation and filtering of vast amounts of information, zeroing in on what is relevant, that leads to intelligence breakthroughs. This was true of the hunt for bin Ladin, which was conducted over a decade and built on the efforts of hundreds, if not thousands, of intelligence officers.

Data collection and analysis are vital tools for preventing terrorist attacks. Terrorist networks rely on a variety of technologies to communicate, to plan operations, and to recruit new personnel. The Government currently makes use of powerful technology to collect and analyze data from communications. Those capabilities will be enhanced as technology advances in the years ahead. As these technical capabilities advance, it will be even more important to define legal parameters that limit these technologies' uses to true needs.

We believe these programs are worth preserving, albeit with additional oversight. Every current or former senior official with whom we spoke told us that the terrorist and cyber threats to the United States are more dangerous today than they were a few years ago. And senior officials explained to us, in clear terms, what authorities they would need to address those threats. Their case is persuasive, and we encountered general agreement about what needs to be done.

Senior leaders must now make this case to the public. The President must lead the Government in an on-going effort to explain to the American people—in specific terms, not generalities—why these programs are critical to the Nation's security. If the American people hear what we have heard in recent months, about the urgent threat and the ways in which data collection is used to counter it, we believe that they will be supportive. If these programs are as important as we believe they are, it is worth making the effort to build a more solid foundation in public opinion to ensure their preservation. While the American public has become more skeptical, now is the time to engage them in an honest, transparent discussion of these issues.

Greater oversight would also help bolster these programs' legitimacy. It imperils public and political support for these programs to limit Classified briefings on their details (and often existence) to only eight leaders in Congress, the "Gang of Eight." All Members of the intelligence oversight committees in the House and Senate should be briefed. The Privacy and Civil Liberties Oversight Board, whose creation was a 9/11 Commission recommendation, is finally functioning, providing an array of well-informed voices on the civil-liberties implications of sensitive National security programs.

INFORMATION SHARING

The 9/11 Commission Report said that the "biggest impediment to all-source analysis—to a greater likelihood of connecting the dots—is the human or systemic resistance to sharing information." Before 9/11, the Government had a weak system for processing and using the vast pool of intelligence information it possessed. One striking example of this inadequacy: In January 2000, the NSA acquired information that could have helped identify one of the eventual hijackers, Nawaf al Hazmi.

This information was not shared with other agencies because no agency made a specific request for it.

Such failures underscore that intelligence sharing among agencies is critically important and will not happen without leadership driving it.

The tone is set at the top. Information sharing has improved significantly since 9/11. There is now a regularly-scheduled meeting on threats convened by the President and attended by the heads of agencies with responsibilities for counterterrorism. The President is directly involved. This forum helps ensure the President is kept up-to-date on threats to the country and what each agency is doing in response. The President's active participation ensures that agencies collaborate (rather than compete) and that they are focused on delivering their best. The meeting also enables senior officials to share information with each other. This valuable practice should be carried over into future administrations.

A major step toward improved information sharing is underway in the form of the Intelligence Community Information Technology Enterprise (ICITE). In this system, the intelligence community will have a single desktop for agencies in the community, providing a common computing environment. Instead of each agency building its own software, which was the practice in the past, the community is implementing an architecture that will be used by all. Authorized users will be able to use common email and related applications. The intelligence community cloud will be privately hosted inside the intelligence community itself, managed under the community's security standards and under the community's security watch.

The National Counterterrorism Center (NCTC), also a 9/11 Commission recommendation, is performing well. NCTC has helped make progress toward instilling a "need-to-share" culture among agencies responsible for counterterrorism, and we have heard that NCTC has received exceptional cooperation from the key intelligence collectors in the Government. In general, we believe that Government officials now recognize that the Government cannot prevent terrorist attacks without bringing together relevant information from many different sources and agencies. Responsibility for making this a reality ultimately rests with managers in each agency: The system must hold accountable every manager with responsibility for sharing information.

One aspect of information sharing is lagging somewhat. "Vertical" sharing—sharing among Federal, State, local, and Tribal officials, as well as the private sector—needs attention. Before 9/11, this form of sharing was woefully inadequate. It has improved substantially since then, but the process is still maturing. It is possible that if Boston authorities had been advised of concerns about Boston Marathon bomber Tamerlan Tsarnaev's interest in connecting with overseas extremist elements, they could have kept a watchful eye on him.

We note, however, that this cannot be a one-way street. State and local law enforcement can also be generators of useful information. The 9/11 hijackers had several encounters with local law enforcement during their time in the United States. Tamerlan Tsarnaev also had several run-ins with the law. At a minimum, State and local law enforcement officials should be trained to recognize the precursors of radicalization.

BIOMETRIC EXIT TRACKING

The 9/11 Commission Report identified terrorists' travel and need for identification documents as vulnerable points in their operations. With the REAL ID Act gradually being implemented by the States, the country is poised to fulfill our recommendation that the Federal Government "set standards for the issuance of birth certificates and sources of identification, such as driver's licenses."

But, as you know, another key recommendation, a biometric exit-tracking system, has still not been implemented, and there is no finish line in sight. Without reliable exit tracking, our Government does not know when a foreign visitor admitted to the United States on a temporary basis has overstayed his or her admission. Had this system been in place before 9/11, we would have had a better chance of detecting the plotters before they struck. Creating an exit-tracking system is a difficult and expensive challenge, but there is no excuse for the fact that 13 years after 9/11 we have neither this capability in place nor a clear plan to get there.

THE CYBER THREAT

Our mandate as a commission was to recommend National security reforms to prevent another 9/11. In our recent conversations with senior National security leaders, however, we encountered another concern over and over again: Intensifying attacks on the country's information systems, in both the private and public sectors.

Over the past decade, cyber threats have grown in scale and intensity, with major breaches at Government agencies and private businesses. The threat emanates largely not from terrorist groups but from traditional state actors such as China, Russia, and Iran. The U.S. Government has confirmed that Chinese-government-backed hackers gained access to more than 2 dozen of America's most advanced weapons systems, including missiles, fighter jets, and advanced ships. In September 2013, Iran hacked into U.S. Navy computer systems. Iran has also been behind cyber attacks on banks and oil companies operating in the Middle East. The Shamoon virus, attributed by many to Iran, infected a key state-owned oil company in Saudi Arabia and left 30,000 computers inoperable.

Non-state actors are also causing increasing damage in the digital world. Sophisticated computer hackers have infiltrated, exploited, and disrupted military, Government, and private-sector systems. Denial-of-service attacks have tied up companies' websites, inflicting serious economic losses. A Russian teenage hacker may have been behind the massive malware attack on the retailer Target, which compromised the credit- and debit-card data of 40 million customers. Increasingly, cyber attacks are targeting smartphones as well. Cyber attacks can constitute another form of asymmetric terrorism. The Syrian Electronic Army is a collection of computer hackers who are loyal to Bashar al-Assad but who operate independently. It has targeted Syrian opposition political groups as well as Western websites. This is the first instance in the Arab world of an organization of civilian cyber experts forming to target groups it deems to be enemies.

Security officials are concerned that terrorist groups' skills in computer technology—and in particular in manipulating offensive cyber capabilities—will increase in the years ahead. Terrorists may also seek to acquire malicious software from adversary nations or from hackers who are proficient at malware coding. This will make an already unpredictable and dangerous cyber realm even more so.

The importance of the internet to American life and to societies across the globe has expanded at a phenomenal rate. As the country becomes ever more dependent on digital services for the functioning of critical infrastructure, business, education, finance, communications, and social connections, the internet's vulnerabilities are outpacing the Nation's ability to secure it. Just as the United States needs to protect its physical infrastructure, so too must we protect the cyber domain.

A growing chorus of senior National security officials describes the cyber domain as the battlefield of the future. Yet, in the words of one former senior leader with whom we spoke, "We are at September 10 levels in terms of cyber preparedness." That needs to change. One lesson of the 9/11 story is that, as a Nation, Americans did not awaken to the gravity of the terrorist threat until it was too late. We must not repeat that mistake in the cyber realm.

Government officials should explain to the public—in clear, specific terms—the severity of the cyber threat and what the stakes are for our country. Public- and private-sector leaders should also explain what private citizens and businesses can do to protect their systems and data.

We support cybersecurity legislation that would enable private companies to responsibly collaborate with the Government in countering cyber threats. Companies should be able to share cyber threat information with the Government without fear of liability.

The U.S. Government can and should do more to deter cyber attacks from state adversaries. The administration should determine and communicate through appropriate channels what the consequences of cyber attacks against us will be, and then act on the basis of those statements. And we should work with our allies to establish norms of cyber space, clearly defining what is considered an attack by one country on another.

The administration and Congress also need to clearly delineate the respective responsibilities of the various agencies in the cyber realm. DHS and other domestic agencies need to complement, rather than attempt to replicate, the technical capabilities of NSA.

WANING SENSE OF URGENCY AMONG THE AMERICAN PEOPLE

One of America's most pressing challenges as a country is to resist the natural urge to relax our guard after 13 years of a draining counterterrorism struggle. In the absence of a major attack, it is easier for some who did not lose loved ones to forget the trauma of 9/11. Increased vigilance has helped us avoid another attack on that scale, but vigilance inevitably wanes over time.

A complacent mindset lulled us into a false sense of security before 9/11. The first World Trade Center bombing in 1993, the East Africa embassy bombings in 1998, and the *Cole* attack in 2000 were warnings of the virulence of the al-Qaeda threat.

But the United States did not do enough. In particular, the Government did not explain to the American people the pattern that was emerging. Without appropriate public understanding, there was insufficient political support for the strenuous counterterrorism efforts that would have been necessary to defeat al-Qaeda.

Avoiding complacency also means taking seriously small things that could be warning signs of something larger beginning to take shape. American officials knew suspicious men were attending flight schools, but in the pre-9/11 mindset it was not considered urgent. Is the April 2013 rifle attack on an electrical substation in Metcalf, California, a harbinger of a more concerted assault on the National electrical grid or another component of critical infrastructure? What might we be missing today that, 3 years from now, will prove to have been a signal, a piece of a larger mosaic?

As we survey the changes in Government made during the last decade, it is evident that the Government has come a long way. But the threat remains very real, and the United States cannot lose focus now. Terrorists can still hurt Americans, abroad and here at home.

To sustain public support for policies and resource levels, National security leaders must communicate to the public—*in specific terms*—what the threat is, how it is evolving, what measures are being taken to address it, why those measures are necessary, and what specific protections are in place to protect civil liberties. In this era of heightened skepticism, generalities will not persuade the public. Leaders should describe the threat and the capabilities they need with as much granularity as they can safely offer.

CONCLUSION

Over the last 13 years, we have damaged our enemy, but the ideology of violent Islamist extremism is alive and attracting new adherents, including right here in our own country.

Our terrorist adversaries and the tactics they employ are evolving rapidly. We will see new attempts, and likely successful attacks. One of our major deficiencies before the 9/11 attacks was that our National security agencies were not adapting quickly enough to the new kind of enemy that was emerging. We must not make that mistake again.

While over the past decade our Government's record in counterterrorism has been good, the terrorist threat will be with us far into the future, demanding that we be ever-vigilant.

Thank you for inviting us to testify, and for this committee's long-standing leadership on these critical issues.

STATEMENT OF JAMIE S. GORELICK, FORMER COMMISSIONER, NATIONAL COMMISSION ON TERRORIST ATTACKS UPON THE UNITED STATES

Ms. GORELICK. Thank you, Tom, and thank you to this committee for this opportunity to appear before you today.

The report points out in general that the Government has done a good job in keeping us safe over the last 10 years. Obviously, we experienced tragedies like the Fort Hood shootings, like the Boston Marathon bombings, but we haven't experienced anything like the attack of 9/11 and its magnitude and its seriousness.

Adding to that, our military and our intelligence capacities have done great damage to core al-Qaeda, particularly to al-Qaeda in Afghanistan, and notably we have killed Osama bin Laden and taken out a good bit of the leadership of core al-Qaeda.

These are very significant achievements. Maybe because of them, we are concerned that the attention of the American people may be drifting away from the threat of terrorism to other problems. I mean, you don't need to watch television for very long to see how many problems and challenges are facing this country. Because we have been mostly safe, the American public may be suffering from a waning sense of urgency, and that may be one of the key observations that we made, that there is not the sense of urgency that there was understandably in the immediate aftermath of 9/11. We have to guard against this sense of complacency, because the threat of terrorism persists and, in many ways, is greater than it was after 9/11.

You have al-Qaeda spin-offs and a metastasis, if you will, of terrorist threats. You have an extremist ideology in which the hatred of the United States is a key part. The groups that have that ideology have proliferated around the world, and al-Qaeda spin-off groups now operate in at least 16 countries around the world.

Of great concern—and I know this committee has looked at this—is the fanatical Islamic State of Iraq and Syria, ISIS, which has conquered much of the territory of western Iraq, slaughtering thousands. That territory expands the sanctuary for terrorists in much the same way that Afghanistan offered sanctuary for al-Qaeda. This increases the threat to the United States and to the West generally.

ISIS has existed for months and years, but its accelerated advances in the recent months have made that area in Iraq and Syria a much more dangerous place, and you can see that just in the last several weeks. You have dozens of Americans, according to the officials with whom we spoke, and maybe thousands of Europeans, who have traveled to Iraq and Syria to join the conflict. The danger is that they may redirect those battlefield skills that they are developing there when they return to our shores or to their home countries.

Al-Qaeda in the Arabian Peninsula also has very advanced bomb-making skills. Those skills are being taught to a new generation of extremists who are fighting in Syria and Iraq, and this poses also a really serious threat to us, particularly a threat to commercial aviation.

Then you have home-grown terrorists, what has been referred to commonly as the lone wolves who have been radicalized over the internet and pose a significant danger. You have, as the Chairman mentioned, Major Hassan who carried out the Fort Hood shootings. You have the Tsarnaev brothers who carried out the Boston Marathon bombing.

We in our recommendations centered on how to protect the country from terrorism. As Tom said, we had these conversations, really, across the board with the people who lead our National security agencies and those who previously held those jobs. We were struck by the persistent concern over cyber and our—and the cyber attacks that are coming both from criminal elements and from foreign countries and from foreign actors to threaten this country, whose National security, after all, sits on a bed of privately-owned enterprise.

The vulnerability of our cyber system, the experience that we have had with vast theft of our intellectual property over the internet, both are really serious internet—really serious National security challenges. The assessment of the people we talked to was that our capacity to fight this threat is lagging behind the threat itself.

We also address in our report—and thank you, Mr. Chairman, for holding it up—we hope that people will avail themselves of it. It is a great deal shorter than our previous report, but we hope no less helpful. We address the NSA's data collection.

In the last 10 years, the scale of data collection has increased dramatically, but it is one of our very best tools in fighting an asymmetric war. Obviously, one needs oversight. One needs protection of civil liberties. But the tools are very, very important. It is incumbent upon Government to explain to the public and persuade the public that these tools are necessary, and we feel that the leadership of this country has failed in that regard, and that the public is more worried about the Government than it is about terrorist enemies who would do us harm.

As the Chairman and the Ranking Member have noted, the Congress has not dealt effectively with the structure of oversight of Homeland Security. The fact that when we made our report calling for more unified oversight, there were 88 committees and now there are 92 committees of oversight is not a good trend. I know you have this chart, but it is worrying that this is what Congressional oversight looks like for the Department of Homeland Security.

On the positive side, the director of National intelligence and the National Counterterrorism Center, we feel, are working very well. We are very pleased with those developments. Information sharing has been much improved. However, the information sharing from the Federal law enforcement agencies to local law enforcement has not been as good as it should be.

As Tom noted, we reflected for a few minutes on how we came to our unanimous conclusions a decade ago. We would just call again on our National leaders for bipartisanship, particularly in the area of our National security.

In many ways, we are safer today than we were a decade ago, but the threat continues. We saw this as a generational struggle, and that struggle goes on, and the greatest danger we fear is that of complacency. We thank you for having this hearing to address these important issues.

Chairman MCCAUL. Thank you, Ms. Gorelick. The Chairman recognizes himself for questions.

I agree, complacency is a danger here, and let me just say again how much I enjoyed our discussion yesterday at the Bipartisan Policy Center. You touched on a lot of the key points that we talked about. I think as we look at the threat, it is evolving. The idea of a large-scale 9/11-style attack probably most likely more difficult to pull off today because we have put a lot of safeguards in place and we have been successful at stopping many of these plots.

However, we did have the Boston bombing. We did have the Fort Hood shooting. We do have al-Qaeda affiliates spreading throughout northern Africa and the Middle East at a rate we have never seen before, owning more territory than they ever have with now-increasing capability and training and money and funding.

So while there is a narrative that, well, bin Laden has been killed and al-Qaeda is sort of on the run, and core al-Qaeda has been decimated by drone strikes, I think that is a dangerous narrative, as well, because I think the threat is not getting less. It is getting probably greater. When that threat grows overseas, so, too, does it to the homeland.

So my first question is, and particularly as we look at ISIS, because I think the Secretary of Homeland Security—I have had very good discussions about the threat coming out of Iraq and Syria now—as being the No. 1 threat to the homeland, and it may not—they are still trying to build bombs to blow up airplanes. They are still a threat to the aviation sector, AQAP, working with al-Nusra, ISIS, obviously, taking the caliphate, talking about hitting the West at some point in time.

This is more of a general question, but how do we protect the United States from these threats?

Mr. KEAN. Well, the threat is absolutely one of the most serious facing us today. We said in our report 10 years ago that if Iraq became a failed state, it went right to the top of the list. Because, remember, when they planned 9/11, it took them 3 or 4 years to do the plot, to do the training, and all of that. We said in our report, they must never again have a place to train and have that kind of security, because if they do, they can again plan a massive assault, like 9/11 on the United States, instead of these worrisome, but minor assaults.

So the idea of ISIS, if it becomes a haven for terrorists—and the same thing, by the way, of Afghanistan after we leave becomes a haven again—that is a great danger to the American homeland. I think we should use every aspect of the United States' power to prevent any terrorist haven from ever, ever being allowed to exist again. There is no greater danger to the American homeland than a haven for terrorists to plot and plan over a number of years.

Chairman MCCAUL. I agree with that.

Ms. Gorelick.

Ms. GORELICK. I would add just two points to that. One is, our greatest resource is intelligence, intelligence gathering about who was there and what their intentions are as to the United States. When you add that to steps taken to prevent people from coming back to the United States or traveling through Europe to the United States on passports that are good for travel here, those are two pretty good protections.

We were speaking earlier about the visa waiver program. The premises of it were that travel from Europe was basically not a threat to the United States. But if people have gone to Iraq and Syria and have gotten the kind of training that Governor Kean has spoken about and can easily travel to the United States after that, that is a threat to us.

Chairman MCCAUL. Thank you for that answer. I would like to refer to a chart, and I had the opportunity to talk about this yesterday, and I am going to continue to talk about this. I am going to the Aspen Institute on Saturday. This will be a great discussion. I think all Members of this committee should know that this is a reality.

[The information follows:]

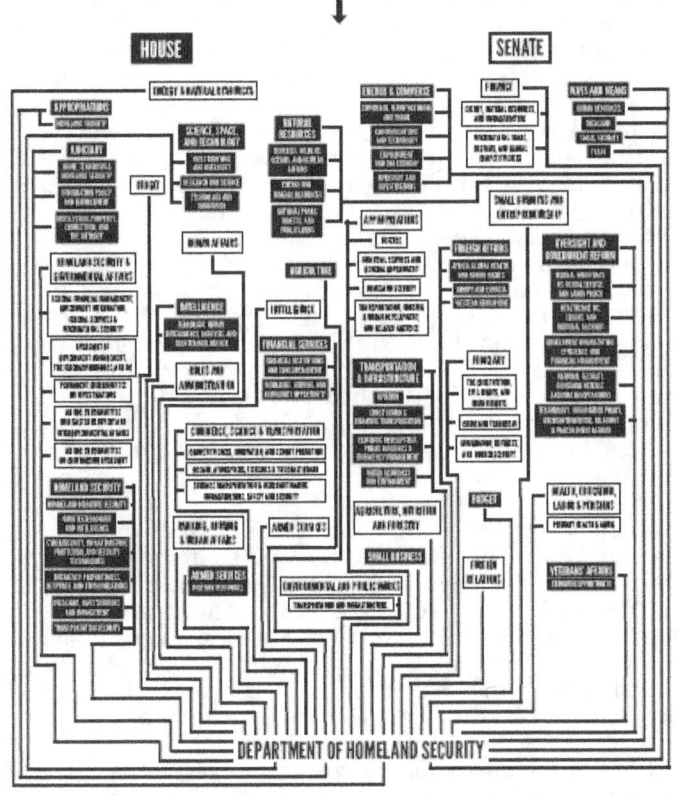

Chairman McCaul. This really defies the No. 1 recommendation of the 9/11 Commission. It was never carried out by Congress. We had the Executive branch consolidate under DHS. If the Congress still continues to silo over jurisdictional battles over who has oversight over the Department of Homeland Security and legislative matters, my concern is not that I am trying to strengthen this committee. What I am concerned about is what this does to the American people and the distraction and detraction that it provides when you have the Secretary having to report to almost 100 committees and subcommittees. Almost 100 in the Congress.

Congress has not done its job in this regard. It takes away from the primary focus on mission that the Department was designed in the first place to do, and that is to protect the American people. This is dysfunction. If you looked in the dictionary and looked under dysfunctional, you would probably see this map in the dictionary.

So my question to you is, as we try to move forward—and I will leverage this commission, I will leverage the victims' families to help us in this effort to change this process once and for all—I know we have two prior Chairmen who tried to do this sitting right here. Unfortunately, they were not successful. I am going to do everything in my power to try to change this.

So what would be your recommendation how to fix this?

Mr. KEAN. Well, look, to begin with, people have got to understand that dysfunctional oversight makes the people of this country less safe, that it impedes the Department in doing its job, that it hurts the Department leadership. We have had four Secretaries now in our Department, two Republicans and two Democrats. All four of them have told me personally and told our group, nothing is more important than changing this and trying to get the oversight right.

The fact they spend 25 percent of their time or more testifying or appearing before a whole myriad of Congressional committees when they should be back in their office protecting the American people is crazy. If you had 100 bosses—think about it. Whatever work you did, if you had 100 bosses, how would you report to them? How would you get your job done? The fact that the Department of Defense, which has this huge responsibility, huge budget, has much less oversight than the Department of Homeland Security, is crazy.

Now, there is nobody—nobody we have ever talked to who doubts this is a problem. There is nobody we would ever talk to who says there shouldn't be a solution to it and Congress shouldn't reform itself in terms of oversight of the Department, no public group, no private group, no Republican group, no Democratic group. Heritage agrees. So does the other—everybody who has looked at it says this is something that ought to be done.

We have been talking about it for a number of years, as a number of you have. You and I both know that the only time they can get done really is at the beginning of the new Congress. It has got—we have got to stop preparing for that now, if it is going to be done.

All I can say is, all 10 of us feel so strongly about it, the families of 9/11 feel so strongly about it, every public group that looks at it feels so strongly about it, whatever we can do to help you get this done, believe me, we will do.

Chairman McCAUL. We appreciate your assistance in that.

Ms. Gorelick, do you have any final words?

Ms. GORELICK. No. That is well said, Tom.

Chairman MCCAUL. Yes, I think that is excellent. Thank you so much for that.

The Chairman now recognizes the Ranking Member.

Mr. THOMPSON. Well, I don't think there is any disagreement with the statement you just made, Governor. It is clear in the minds of everyone who is—as this Chairman said, that two former Chairs agree wholeheartedly that jurisdiction is important, and because we don't, as a country, we are less safe. I look forward to working with this Chairman, as the Ranking Member, to get as much of that chart reduced to reality as possible.

So with that, there have been a couple of incidents that come up. The Snowden incident, we learned some things from it. But also, it has created some real harm with traditional allies. How do you think we need to fix situations like that, Governor, so that those countries that we rely on for intelligence and information sharing, that we make sure that we keep that?

Mr. KEAN. What I believe in—my personal point of view—and I think the point of view, really, of all of us on the commission—is that we think there should be a greater degree of openness with the American people. I believe personally that everything has changed, in terms of the terror threat, the technology, all of that. That requires a different response from Government, but I believe the Government in a democracy has a duty to the American people to say, all right, this is the problem and these are the methods we are planning to use to deal with this problem.

That involves, obviously, also talking about who gets information and what their qualifications are, whether the contractors that are hired by the Government are using the proper means to make sure that only the people with a need to know get only the information they need to know.

But in general, American people were surprised by this. I know a lot because of our work on 9/11 and since, I was surprised by it. Maybe some of you were surprised by it. I don't know how deeply what we were doing was shared even with this committee.

It is not enough in my opinion to share it with the Gang of Eight. I think not everything—how we do everything, but the idea of what we are trying to do and why we are trying to do it, the more broadly we share that with the American people, the more the American people will support us.

We need to share. We need to gather this information. We know we have to do it in order to trap the kind of terrorists that attacked this country. But if you do it as a surprise and let it be leaked by a person like Snowden, then the American people are blindsided. Then you have got all sorts of people worried about why the Government is looking at them, why they need this information, because they were surprised.

So my—you know, my recommendation is that, as widely as possible, trust the American people. If they understand the danger, they will understand the need for the solutions. But if you don't trust the American people and try to do everything in secret and then they find out about it, they are not going to trust the American Government again.

So, anyway, my recommendation would be just getting new problems out there, the terrorists are trying to attack us in new ways, the cyber threat is very real, so the methodologies we have to use to fight that threat have got to change, but we are telling the American people what we are doing ahead of time and why we are doing it.

Mr. THOMPSON. Well, and thank you, Governor. You talked toward the end about the cyber threat. Ms. Gorelick, this committee is trying to get some of its tentacles around this issue. We have pushed legislation out.

What do you think DHS's role in the cybersecurity discussion ought to be?

Ms. GORELICK. Thank you, Ranking Member Thompson, for that question. This is an issue that I have been working on since the early to mid-1990s. It is not a new problem. One of the critical issues is the relationship between the resources that we have on the intelligence and military side versus the resources and responsibilities that we have domestically. Since that time, of course, we have had the advent of the Department of Homeland Security.

No. 1, I don't think the Department of Homeland Security can replicate the resources at NSA. NSA is world-class. We can't build two of them. So the question then becomes, what are the authorities that the Department of Homeland Security itself needs? I would ask the Secretary what authority he needs when he is the one directing the activities of NSA domestically.

We did not discuss this as a commission, so I am just going to give you my personal view. I think that the Department of Homeland Security has to bring to bear the awareness that it has of our domestic vulnerabilities and the relationships with our domestic industry. But the resources have to remain in NSA.

Making sure that we have a well-oiled machine in that regard is extremely, extremely important. I would run a tabletop with the two parts of Government to make sure that they are really working smoothly in that regard.

Mr. THOMPSON. Thank you. I yield back, Mr. Chairman.

Chairman MCCAUL. The Chairman recognizes Dr. Broun from Georgia.

Mr. BROUN. Thank you, Mr. Chairman.

A lot has changed. A lot hasn't changed since y'all's commission put out your report 10 years ago. I appreciate the update from y'all's commission. I think it is extremely important.

But I want to go to two issues that you did not talk about during your original testimony. One of those is border security, and the other one is the visa waiver that Ms. Gorelick mentioned just briefly, which I blame four administrations, frankly, for not securing the border. The four administrations, two Republican and two Democrats now, have refused to obey the law that was put on the books in 1986 under the Reagan administration to deal with illegal aliens in this country to secure our border.

Right now, we have a flood of illegal aliens coming into this country. We see on the TV all these kids which is a flood of these unaccompanied alien children, UACs, coming into this country, but that is just a small segment of people who are coming across our border. Would you all agree with me that it is absolutely imperative for our own National security for us to do everything that we can to make sure that anybody who comes in this country is vetted and brought in this country legally?

Mr. KEAN. Yes.

Mr. BROUN. What could we do to secure our border? What kind of recommendations would you make? I think we ought to put the National Guard on the borders, north and south, and do everything we can to electronically monitor, to use drones, to use every asset that we have to secure the borders. But I see this as a huge National security issue, because there are a lot of people coming across the border today that are OTMs, other than Mexicans. We know they are coming from the Middle East, they are coming from Africa, places like Somalia, where we have a tremendous growth of groups that want to destroy our country.

Mr. KEAN. Yes, as a group, we didn't talk about border security. We have had recommendations, for instance, that REAL ID, which is when somebody is in this country, they should have an ID that can't be copied. States—we ask States be required to do the driver's licenses so that they can't be duplicated so easily for illegal purposes. That was one of the problems of 9/11, that all these people who were in this country to do damage to us had phony IDs that were duplicated.

Another thing we recommended is that even the people who are allowed to come legally, we don't know when they leave. So, for instance, the 9/11 hijackers overstayed their welcome. They overstayed their visa times, and we didn't know it. We still don't know it.

If somebody comes in, we know how to let them in, but we don't know how long they stay. We don't know how many people are here illegally because their visas have run out. That is a couple of our recommendations that are still pending in the area of security, of who is in this country.

But border security is something we—obviously, very important, this committee has addressed it. People are talking about it a lot. But it is not something that we talked about a lot within our commission this time. We simply didn't have the resources at the time to do the investigation.

Mr. BROUN. I hope our current Congress and administration will insist that we secure our border, because it is actually a tremendous security problem. I want to go to something that Ms. Gorelick mentioned earlier, and I think that I agree with what she said, and that is about the Visa Waiver Program.

I think we have a marked change in the environment in Europe and in countries that we allow visa waivers. We are allowing people to come in this country under the Visa Waiver Program. Would you both agree that we must change—or, I think, end the Visa Waiver Program and stop the ability for people coming in this country that want to do harm to Americans?

Ms. GORELICK. I don't know enough to say that it needs to be stopped. We—as the Governor said—didn't have investigative authority. We just were able to talk to individuals within the Government and formerly within the Government who were kind enough to share their time and their thoughts with us.

But it does strike us as a pertinent inquiry to ask whether the premises of the original program are still correct and, if they are not, whether there needs to be any adjustment to the program. Because as I recall, the premises of the program were that these Western countries, whose citizens we allow to come into the United States with minimal procedures, were safe, they had strong processes for themselves, protecting against terrorism, and thus to enhance travel among those countries and the United States. We would have a Visa Waiver Program.

Well, if you have people carrying passports, which allow them simply to get on a plane and come to the United States, who are fighting with ISIS in Iraq and Syria, perhaps the premise of that program is no longer correct. I would ask the question, because I think it is a pertinent one.

Mr. BROUN. Thank you. Mr. Chairman, my time is expired, and I think you all for being here. But until we secure our borders, until we know who is here, and we start enforcing the laws, nothing else matters, in my opinion, Mr. Chairman. I yield back. Thank you.

Chairman McCAUL. Chairman recognizes Ms. Clarke from New York.

Ms. CLARKE. Thank you, Mr. Chairman. Thank you both so much for being here and sharing with us your wealth of knowledge.

I want to circle back to the questions around the sort of breach of confidence in the American people with the unearthing of the NSA scandals. I am sure you are familiar with the controversy surrounding NSA's bulk collection and metadata programs. The Privacy and Civil Liberties Oversight Board found that these programs were illegal.

Could you give us a bit more of your thoughts, given the uptick of lone wolf terrorist attacks? It seems as if it is necessary for more funding and training to go into local law enforcement and not to large-scale data programs. Why should Congress rely on the NSA's metadata collection program as a way to prevent a lone-wolf attack?

Ms. GORELICK. Sure. The data programs are, in my personal view, and I think in the view of the commission, fundamental to the safety of the United States. That is not to say that they should not be subject to strict oversight to protect the civil liberties of our citizens. They should be. The need for them should, as Governor Kean has said, be explained to the American people.

When you are carrying out an asymmetric war, where a lone wolf can do tremendous damage, or 19 people can do horrendous damage, one of the best tools that you have is the collection of information. My worry about the Snowden revelations is that they undermine the faith of the American people in our National security activities.

I think those activities are important. I think the case has to be made for them. I think that people need to be reassured that some of the things that have been said about them are not true, and to the extent that there remain worries, there need to be safeguards put in place, but I personally—and I think the commission feels this, as well—feel that it is critically important that we maintain the ability to do surveillance and analysis to track people who would do us harm.

Ms. CLARKE. I think the—breaking down the whole metadata into more simplistic terminology for Americans then makes a distinction, because certainly we are concerned about our right to privacy. But folks are not clear on what metadata actually is. I think that that has caused a bit of the consternation that we are all feeling.

Ms. GORELICK. If I might say one other thing about that, the reluctance of the intelligence community to talk about these programs actually did the programs a great deal of harm. Because when the report first came out on the so-called PRISM program, for example, it suggested that there was a big vacuum cleaner at the back of Google and Facebook that took all communications and fed it to the Federal Government. Well, that is not true. But the truth of what the program is and is not never caught up with the original stories.

Mr. KEAN. I would say, we talked a little bit about the public's fatigue in some ways with this issue and their lack of attention these days. I think the two are tied together. I think at the very highest levels of this Government, the public has got to be informed of what the threat is today, not what it was 10 years ago, what it is today and how serious that threat is.

Then, along with that, they have got to be told what and why we are doing to protect the American people, because there is all sorts of confusion out there. I mean, this committee knows, but the people don't. I mean, I get the darnedest questions, and you probably do, too. People have no idea what this is all about. They do think that people are following them around with cameras or snooping on their phone messages or emails. They are not.

Ms. CLARKE. So——

Mr. KEAN. We have got to tell the American people that, but tell them what we are doing and why we are doing it, and it is to protect them, because this is what the threat is. I just—I think that is—at this point, it has got to come from the highest levels.

Ms. CLARKE. So just quickly—I have got 4 seconds—can DHS play a greater role in the intelligence community?

Mr. KEAN. Well, DHS has got a bit of a different role. It has got to cooperate totally with the intelligence community. It has got to be a seamless web. The importance of DHS to me is that I think even if the threat is just a lone wolf, maybe even if it is a bigger threat, it is probably not going to be stopped by a member of the FBI. It is probably going to be stopped by some local law enforcement or maybe even just a private citizen.

I mean, it struck me that in that attempt to bomb Times Square, Times Square, there are more police per square inch than any place else in the world. Yet who was the one who discovered it? It was a street vendor who reported it. When he reported it, then the action went right back up. That is what is going to happen again.

So people—DHS makes the connections with the local community, and that has got to be seamless. That is—we are not there yet. We are—thanks to our recommendations in part, the vertical sharing of information is now pretty good, much better than it was.

But the horizontal is not as good as it ought to be, and it has got to be a lot better to protect the American people.

Ms. CLARKE. Thank you. Yield back.

Chairman MCCAUL. Thank you. Mr. Palazzo is recognized.

Mr. PALAZZO. Thank you, Mr. Chairman. I want to thank the witnesses for being here. Enjoying hearing your testimony. I want to elaborate on something the Chairman started off with in his opening statements and I think followed up with some of his questions, and it is about Congressional reform.

I think that is too important just to skip over really briefly. I think it is—and so I would like to just go over some of the statements that we have from the 9/11 Commission recommendation. Congress should create a single, principal point of oversight and review for homeland security. Congressional oversight for intelligence and counterterrorism is now dysfunctional.

Well, a lot of people think Congress is dysfunctional. I think the more people that find out that this—that the Department of Homeland Security has to report to over 119 committees, subcommittees, caucuses, and commissions, they are going to realize the answer to why we are dysfunctional is because we can't even, you know, focus on homeland security.

I have every confidence in the Chairman, in the Ranking Member, that this—that homeland security affairs need to be centralized in this committee and this committee alone.

Secretary Chertoff has stated that committees that have no homeland security focus risk directing DHS agencies in a way that conflicts with broader National security strategy. Of course, you know, everybody on this committee I think agrees.

The most pressing is former Homeland Security Secretary Tom Ridge stated, oversight is the duty of Congress. It is your responsibility and is an absolute—absolutely necessary. But the current number of Congressional committees with homeland security jurisdiction is not oversight. It is overkill.

So I would like to open that, you know, Congressional reform questioning back to you to—for you to be able to take the time that you need to expand on it. How can we fix it? Hopefully, going into the 114th Congress, leadership will realize how important it is we got to pull, you know, whatever the—and, also, I guess, whatever the obstacles are, we have to eliminate them.

Maybe you could share your thoughts on what those obstacles are, as well.

Mr. KEAN. Well, we made 41 recommendations, broadly supported by the American people as a whole and by this Congress. Forty of them have been implemented in whole or in part, 40 of them. One is outstanding, and only one. It stands there glaring, really, as the one thing that hasn't been done to protect the American people, and it is the United States Congress.

The Congress was wonderful. You know, the Congress got together and reorganized the intelligence department, passed a whole series of laws, worked—except for the one affecting Congress.

I haven't found anybody outside of Congress or, frankly, inside of Congress who disagrees with the recommendation. I haven't found anybody standing up and saying, yeah, there should be 90 committees. I mean, there is no argument there. No single person anywhere that I have found in leadership, out of leadership that has said that is not the right thing to do.

But they don't do it. That is what is so frustrating to us and frustrating to everybody who has looked at it. I say, when people from the right, people from the left, people from the center all say the same thing is important to preserve National security in this country, they expect it to be done. Ten years, got worse.

Ms. GORELICK. What you could have happen is the next disaster. After the next disaster, someone will ask, who in Congress was in charge? Who was performing the oversight? As much as the title of this committee would suggest that it is, the reality that you will have is that dozens of committees are. Everyone knows that when everyone is in charge, no one is. But it would be too bad if it takes another disaster to make that point.

Mr. PALAZZO. Well, that was well said. I do hope leadership gets a copy of the testimony here today, Mr. Chairman, that we can hopefully change that going into the 114th Congress. Real quick. Cyber attacks, some people say that is America's biggest National security threat. Your testimony highlights that we are at pre-9/11 mindset when it comes to cybersecurity. What is your assessment of the U.S. Government, and particularly DHS, evolving capabilities to mitigate against and attack against Government computer networks, but also maybe private-sector assets, such as our grid, our satellites, and other things?

Mr. KEAN. We talked to every leader, I think, in this Government with major responsibilities for National security, plus a number of those who are no longer in Government but still involved. Every single one of them said we are not doing what we should be doing to protect ourselves against cybersecurity. Because this stealing of information is so invisible to the American public, they don't realize what a disaster it is. They don't understand that we are losing the capacity to develop some weapons systems or they are being stolen by other countries. They don't know that some of our technology which could create great jobs in this country and are important for our defense is being stolen today as we sit here, because it is silent.

I think Government, businesses don't always like to admit they have been robbed in a cyber way. So we don't read about it, and the public isn't really informed on it. But I think the leaders we talk to, I think that was probably their biggest concern that we were way behind in putting together an approach to cyber, and in a number of ways, No. 1 in the Government itself and, No. 2, the Congress had not yet been able to get together on a cyber bill.

Ms. GORELICK. I would add two things. One is, you asked both about the defense of Governmental computers and also about the private sector. I think the Government is doing much better at protecting itself and its own systems than it is helping the private sector protect itself. I think, I think we think—our vulnerability in the latter area is greater.

Now, this is hard, because having the Department of Defense, for example, defending a telephone system, a power grid, a transportation system, a banking system in a way that it would defend itself has all kinds of complexities to it. It is hard.

I will just say one thing. I did a mock tabletop that was on CNN. It was organized by former Secretary Chertoff. He played the role of the National security adviser, and he asked me to play the role of the attorney general. I asked him ahead of time whether—you know, if he could tell me what legal issues he thought would emerge so that I could prepare, and he said, oh, don't worry about it. This is not so much about legal issues.

As the hypothetical unfolded in this exercise, everyone, before they acted, would ask me, as the mock attorney general, can I do this? I think that the issue of what the authorities of our Government agencies are to come to the aid of a system under attack is still a very much live question and may be one of the hardest in this country, because we are uncomfortable with having our National security apparatus operating in the private sector.

But if you think about what the real threats are, an enemy who would shut down our power grid, for example, those are real threats to which I don't believe we have great answers at the moment. I would press our leaders on this, and I would ask the hard questions. I think you are right to focus on this.

Mr. PALAZZO. Thank you. Thank you, Mr. Chairman. Yield back.

Chairman MCCAUL. Chairman recognizes Mr. O'Rourke.

Mr. O'ROURKE. Thank you, Mr. Chairman. Governor Kean, Ms. Gorelick, thank you for your public service, your testimony today. So much of what you advised us on in your initial report and in this reprise this year resonate, obviously, with this committee, most importantly the concentration of jurisdiction, responsibility, and oversight. That makes so much common sense, it is hard to argue with. I don't know why we haven't been able to do it, but, you know, we will add my efforts to the cause to ensure that it happens.

I wanted to—because the issue of border security was raised, I wanted to touch upon it, welcome your comments on it, should you like to. If not, I would also like to ask you about your recommendations related to the authorization and use of military force.

But when it comes to border security, I want to make sure that we don't conflate problems and mislead and misdirect the public and policymakers. By any measure today, the Southern Border is as secure as it has ever been. If you look at apprehensions, on the eve of 9/11, in 2000, we had 1.6 million apprehensions at our Southern Border. Last year, it was 420,000. This year, given the spike in refugees and asylum-seekers from Central America, it may come close to 500,000, but it is still a fraction of what it was 15 years ago on the eve of 9/11.

I represent El Paso, Texas. The committee is sick of hearing me say this, but I want to make sure I get it out in front of you. It is the safest city of America 4 years in a row, despite being the largest binational community in the world, conjoined with Ciudad Juárez in Mexico.

The National Guard, drones, border fencing, none of those would have stopped the 9/11 terrorists. As you have said in your answer to my colleague earlier, that was really an issue of visa overstays and ensuring that we understand who is in this country, how long they are here, what they are doing, and when they depart. So I wanted to kind-of clear the record on whether or not the border is secure.

On the issue of the authorization and use of military force, I would love to understand more specifically what you are thinking about. You know, I—along with my constituents—are wary with the number of years that we have been at war, the lives lost, the treasure spent, and the inconclusive results, whether you look at Iraq, whether you look at Afghanistan, what did we purchase with those lives and that money?

Yet you can't ignore the threat that ISIL poses to us, should they gain control of the levers of a state, a functioning state, and be able to issue passports, be able to print currency, have those protections that statehood offers. What is your advice on how we move forward with this authorization? What would you recommend to us to ensure that we are safeguarding the homeland's interests and yet not committing ourselves to perpetual war?

Mr. KEAN. What is difficult is that the administration in action is relying on a resolution that was passed for a specific purpose a long time ago. It has never been revisited.

I am a historian by training. I believe very, very strongly that the Congress has a very important role when it comes to whether or not this country should commit troops. It should never give up that role. It should fight for it.

I worry very much that, as long as we just let that resolution sit out there and let this administration—future administration use that instead of coming to an understanding of what Congress's role and what the administration role is and doing it openly, that we are going to get ourselves in trouble.

It is a hard one. It is very, very hard. I understand why people feel they would rather not deal with it. But when you commit American forces and American lives, very, very important that Congress has got to have a role that everybody understands. I don't think they do right now.

Mr. O'ROURKE. Jamie.

Ms. GORELICK. I would just add a couple of thoughts. One is that I don't think the current actions of the Executive branch are legally vulnerable for relying on the current authorization. But it is better policy for there to be a debate about what we should and should not be doing as a country.

Congress, as Tom says, has a very important role here. The debate, if you have it, will be a hard one, because there will be people who say, enough is enough, we don't want to do anything, we are done. There will be people who say, the threat is very real, we can't unilaterally back off from the fight, and here are the authorities that we need. It is a hard argument. It will be a tough argument. But it is an argument that should be had. It might actually help to explain to the American people what the current threat is.

Our view is that it is sort of in many ways out of sight, out of mind. Given that we are sending troops to be in harm's way, given that our intelligence community resources are putting themselves, those people in harm's way, it would be a very helpful discussion for Congress to have.

Mr. O'ROURKE. Great. Thank you. Mr. Chairman, I yield back.

Chairman McCAUL. The Chairman recognizes Mrs. Brooks.

Mrs. BROOKS. Thank you, Mr. Chairman, and thank you, it was wonderful to visit with you right before the hearing. So thank you so very much for being here.

In your report, you did talk about something that I want to shift gears a little bit, the possibility of a major biological attack that in terms of the numbers killed and the psychological impact that it would have, that it would be so devastating.

I chair the Emergency Preparedness, Response, and Communications Subcommittee, and we have had a couple of hearings on—and actual briefings on the threat of a biological attack. We believe that that is a very real possibility. We also know and heard from testimony from Dr. Bob Cadlick and Tom Ingelsby that the threat is very real. We had a hearing on that.

But the administration has eliminated the position of special assistant to the president and senior director for biodefense policy, a position that did exist in the Bush administration. I am wondering your thoughts on whether or not there is sufficient attention and focus on the possibility of a biological attack, again, one of those types of attacks that I think the American people truly have no real understanding of.

Are we doing—what should we be doing to better educate the public and even Members of Congress and the country about what that means, what we should be doing, the importance of tools like BioWatch, and the importance of those investments? Anything— and particularly after we have seen what has happened in Syria, with Assad, and now that we know we have so many Westerners, you know, possibly, you know, in Iraq and Syria. You know, what kind of concern and attention should we be giving to biological?

Mr. KEAN. Biological—to deal with some of these things without scaring the American people to death is sometimes difficult. But we always said about biological the same thing we said about nuclear, really. We didn't think it was the most likely, but the results if it was successful would be so devastating that we had to do everything in our power on the preventative side from educating the American people, which I don't think we are doing sufficiently in that area, to doing whatever we can do in Government to prepare, both unfortunately, to prepare in two ways. One is around educate the American people to prevent it. The other is, God forbid it should ever happen, are we prepared medically to deal with the after-effects? Are we doing enough? Probably not.

But it is a difficult, difficult subject to deal with, with the American people, I think, anyway.

Ms. GORELICK. A low-probability, high-consequence event, very much worried us in our first report. We remain concerned about it and very much appreciate, Congresswoman Brooks, that you are spending so much time on this, as are others, the Center for Biosecurity and others.

We don't know—we did not have the resources to look into whether the Executive branch is properly organized on this. We do know that there are a lot of people who are looking at it. It is my impression that on the resilience that Tom referred to, the preparedness for an event, we are in much better shape. You could see that in part in how well-organized the medical community was in

Boston in the aftermath of the marathon bombing to respond. I think the medical community has actually made great strides.

But what we are doing to prevent such an event, what our surveillance is of pathogens and the like, we just don't know, but it remains with us a very persistent worry.

Mrs. BROOKS. The only other question I would like to ask is what your observations are about—and, again, this is what our committee is focused on—our interoperable communications issues. With FirstNet standing up and finally getting started, any closing—and my time I have remaining—any thoughts you would like to talk about, the level of interoperable communication success or lack thereof?

Mr. KEAN. It was one of our biggest frustrations that that recommendation took so long. People, as you know, died on 9/11 because policemen couldn't talk to firemen. People died in Katrina because people in helicopters couldn't talk to people in boats because these things weren't—and I know we have now got something finally in place, but I would suggest the function of this committee and the Congress is to monitor that very, very carefully and make sure it is being carried out not just in certain regions, but all over the country in a way that first responders, emergency management can talk to each other, because that is—that saves lives, not just in terrorist attacks, but in hurricanes and floods and all sorts of other emergencies.

I would just—that is—we haven't got the power to do it as citizens, but as a committee, I would ask you please to monitor that as carefully as possible and make sure it is done the way it was supposed to be done.

Ms. GORELICK. I would second that.

Mrs. BROOKS. Well, thank you. Pleased to share, we are having a hearing, Ranking Member Payne and I are having a hearing on—in early September after the recess on FirstNet and its progress and where we need to go. So thank you. Thanks for all you have done for the country. Yield back.

Chairman MCCAUL. It is a good transition to Mr. Payne.

Mr. PAYNE. Thank you, Mr. Chairman, to the Ranking Member. It is a real honor and a privilege to have one of the greater Governors that the State of New Jersey ever had the fortune of serving the State, contributed in many ways to our State and to our Nation.

I think the statute of limitations has run out, so I can say that I voted for Governor Kean in his second term.

[Laughter.]

Mr. PAYNE. I am not supposed to say that, but it is a testimony to his dedication and commitment to all the citizens of the State of New Jersey and for this country, so we thank you.

Mr. KEAN. Thank you.

Mr. PAYNE. Defending our homeland relies on, you know, effective information sharing, as we were just talking about, because various intelligence agencies and also from our international partners. Since 9/11, how has information sharing improved in the intelligence community? Where is there significant room for improvement? Can DHS play a greater role in the intelligence community?

Mr. KEAN. Well, information sharing is a lot better, a lot better, particularly across agencies. As you know, some of us believe that 9/11 might have been prevented if the intelligence agencies had shared information they had, because it would have resulted in the apprehension of at least some of the terrorists and that might have disrupted the plot. So it is very, very important.

We believe since this Congress established the DNI, and the DNI is still a very new part of Government, but what we gain from talking to people across a wide variety of Government agencies is the confidence that DNI is finally working, that it seems to be coordinating the way we intended when we wrote the report and the Congress intended when they passed the bill and that it is coming into its own. That was very, very encouraging.

I would say the problem on sharing, I think—and this is homeland security—is vertical sharing, whether or not people in the Federal Government trust people at the local level, because they have to. That is—if there isn't that shared trust, if the State policemen, the local policemen, the local agencies aren't sharing information with the Federal Government back and forth on a matter of trust, then we are not going to ever protect ourselves properly.

So is the sharing much better? Yes. Is the sharing vertically, particularly with the local level what it should be? No. I think Homeland Security has got to continually work on that.

Mr. PAYNE. Ms. Gorelick.

Ms. GORELICK. I would just add a couple of things. As Governor Kean said, the director of national intelligence has done a very good job of deciding the rules of the road with respect to sharing. The National Counterterrorism Center has become the fulcrum that one wants to see. So we have broken down silos across the Government.

There has to be wide sharing of information of counterterrorism information, and it has to move very quickly. The challenge is to make sure that people who don't need to know certain facts, certain information don't get that, and that is the next stage of development that has to occur here, because otherwise you get a Snowden or a Bradley Manning, which is a terrible threat to our National security to have somebody who doesn't need to know taking that information and proliferating it.

So we are very pleased with what we have seen in the progress that the DNI has made and the NCTC. We think there is yet progress to be made in informing State and local police and other first responders in communities so that they can be of help, as well.

Mr. PAYNE. Mr. Chairman, in the interest of time, I will yield back. Thank you.

Chairman McCAUL. Thank you, sir.

Mr. Barletta is recognized.

Mr. BARLETTA. Thank you, Mr. Chairman.

As you know, the 9/11 Commission Report makes several connections between enforcement of our immigration laws and National security. Page 98 of the report describes how terrorists would inevitably benefit from any form of legal status. Terrorists fear deportation, and they don't care about American citizenship. They simply need to find a legal way to remain in the United States.

Another section of the 9/11 Commission report describes the importance of enforcing the immigration laws Congress has already passed, such as the establishment of an exit system to track visa overstays. The report describes how INS, now CPB, initiated but failed to bring to completion two efforts that would have provided inspectors with information relevant to counterterrorism, a proposed system to track foreign student visa compliance, and a program to establish a way of tracking travelers' entry to and exit from the United States.

The report urged full implementation of a biometric exit system. The report also describes how border security should not be seen as a bargaining chip in immigration reform, but rather a significant National security concern. The report states, indeed, after 19 hijackers demonstrated the relative ease of obtaining a United States visa and gaining admission into the United States, border security still is not considered a cornerstone of National security policy. We believe that it must be made one.

The 9/11 Commission further noted on page 390 of its report that all but one of the 9/11 hijackers acquired some form of United States identification document, some by fraud. As a result, the commission recorded that the Federal Government should set standards for the issuance of birth certificates and sources of identification, such as driver's license.

Now, Governor Kean, why do you think the Department of Homeland Security continues to drag its feet in completing the biometric exit system? What kinds of threats continue to slip through the crack as a result?

Mr. KEAN. Well, part of it, frankly, is just enforcing the laws we have. Sixteen of the 19 terrorists came in with some form of phony visa or phony identification. Then, of course, as you say, they easily got driver's licenses and credit cards and all of that, and they were roaming around this country, even though some of them were wanted in other parts of the world. A lot of that has been corrected.

We believe still, very strongly, in the biometric system. My understanding is, the resistance has come from certain States. There are a number of States who have done it. A number of the driver's licenses we now carry are biometrically done and would stand up against any kind of scrutiny, but certain States have not yet, I don't think, done it yet, and I would encourage us to make them comply with the law like they are supposed to do it.

So it is a—and everything we said in the report I think we still stand by today. We are not where we should be still. We have done a lot. Most of our recommendations have been fulfilled in part or in full, which you mentioned some of them that haven't been and we still stand by them.

Mr. BARLETTA. Yes, I quote the 9/11 Commission Report often, because it was passed by Congress, signed by the President, is law, but yet we continue to ignore it, whether it is the States offering driver's license to people who are undocumented, and undocumented means we don't know who they are. They don't have documentations.

Mr. KEAN. Yes.

Mr. BARLETTA. So we are issuing a legal form for people to exist here in the United States without really knowing who they are.

Even when we talk about immigration reform, again, that violates the concept of that report, because of the fraudulent documents, and we don't know who we are allowing to stay here. Without border security first—you know, any State that has an international airport is a border State, in my opinion, because people can easily—and nearly 50 percent of the people that are here illegally didn't cross the border. They come on a visa.

Mr. KEAN. Yes, and we would also, again, recommend you look at this—you look at finding a way to track people who overstay the visas, because that is what the terrorists did.

Mr. BARLETTA. Or method of entry for people that want to hurt us.

Mr. KEAN. We had no idea that they were still here, because we have no way of seeing how long people stay in this country.

Mr. BARLETTA. So a true border security bill won't be a true border security bill unless we implement a biometric entry and exit so that we know everyone that—whether they are coming or going in the country, because just simply at our physical borders, north and south, isn't enough.

Mr. KEAN. It is not enough. You are right.

Mr. BARLETTA. Thank you. Thank you, Mr. Chairman. Yield back.

Chairman MCCAUL. The Chairman recognizes Mr. Barber.

Mr. BARBER. Thank you, Mr. Chairman.

I want to thank the witnesses, not only for your testimony today, but also for the important patriotic duty that you performed as members of the commission and now to give us an update on progress on the 10th anniversary of your initial findings and report.

I want to talk about a few issues that we have discussed in part, but a couple we haven't. First of all, when the Chairman showed the chart illustrating the lines of responsibility that subcommittees and committees have over Department of Homeland Security, it was for me the first graphic depiction of what we have been talking about since I got here in 2012.

Unbelievable. I saw that in the *Times* on Sunday and I thought, somebody is trying to make a point, and they made it really well, because look at this chart. We have to get to the bottom of this. Congress—this Congress, obviously, won't do it. No time left. But I believe it is an essential priority and charge of—when the Congress comes back into session in 2014.

Do you have any estimate at all—does anybody have an estimate of the number of hours that the Department of Homeland Security must put in to answering the questions from over 100 different organizations, entities, and committees? Do you know that?

Mr. KEAN. Somebody talked about it today, didn't they?

Ms. GORELICK. Well, we know the number of hearings and the number of responses. I think actually the Chairman had that in his opening statement.

But I think it is both the amount of time and effort that the leadership of the Department of Homeland Security is putting in, but it is also the lack of an appropriate counterparty. When I was deputy attorney general, I knew very well what the Chairman and Ranking Member in the House and the Senate of my authorizing committees thought about what I was doing. If I didn't know, I knew who to call.

If I had to have that same interaction with even five committees, it would have been disabling. As Governor Kean said earlier, anyone who has had more than one boss knows that that is disabling. It is the lack of cohesion in the interaction with the Executive branch that undermines agility. If we have learned anything since 9/11, it is the need for agility.

Mr. BARBER. I agree with you. I think the Department cannot be as nimble as it needs to be to meet the homeland security issues that are coming up every day in new ways. This committee, I think, has done an incredibly good job of coming together in a very bipartisan way. Since I have been here, we have had markups with 100 percent unanimity amongst the committee Members. We are really focused.

Pretty much like on the other committee I am on, the Department of Homeland Security's committee, Homeland—the House Armed Services Committee, has the same attitude, the same knowledge, the same focus on making sure DOD is accountable. This Congress cannot perform its duties of oversight with all of these jurisdictions in place, and I hope that the new Congress will take this up as a priority.

I want to talk a little bit about border security. My colleague, Mr. O'Rourke, did indicate that some areas of the border, particularly the area that he represents, are certainly more secure than they have ever been. I accept that. But there are gaps.

One of those gaps, unfortunately, is in a district that I represent, where 83 miles of border with Mexico is not secure. Other than— the ports of entry are pretty well-staffed, but when you get out into the rugged areas where the ranchlands are, it is wide-open territory.

I believe that not only is it wide-open territory for the cartels, who are smuggling people and drugs, it is a potentially wide open territory for potential terrorist movement across our Southern Border with whatever devices they want to harm the country. Would you comment on that aspect of border security? I will just give you one statistic about my district, the sector that is in my district: 47 percent of the drugs that are seized in this country are seized in the Tucson sector, 47 percent. Thirty-five percent of the illegal immigrants are seized or apprehended in my district.

It seems to me that is wide open for terrorist activity. Would you comment on how we might address that issue, since clearly we have to defend the homeland against that possibility?

Ms. GORELICK. You know, this is—we are private citizens and had no investigative resources, so we did not study the issue of the relationship between the border today and the potential for a terrorist threat. We did spend, as Governor Kean has said, a lot of time in our original report on the importance of securing our borders and ensuring that we know who is in this country.

But beyond that, we did the work that 10 people with a little bit of funding and a willingness of people in the National security community to talk to us can do. So I don't know that we can give you a current assessment ourselves.

Mr. KEAN. We had—all of our staff was volunteer. We, of course, are all volunteers. We didn't have either the security clearances or the money and staff to do the kind of work which I think you would have liked to do, to answer your question.

Mr. BARBER. Well, I certainly want to thank the witnesses. I am over my time, but you have done an incredible job serving this country today and in your original work on the commission. Thank you, Mr. Chairman. I yield back.

Chairman MCCAUL. The Chairman recognizes Mr. Marino.

Mr. MARINO. No questions.

Chairman MCCAUL. The Chairman recognizes Mr. Meehan.

Mr. MEEHAN. Thank you, Chairman.

Thank you, Governor, for being here. I am Pat Meehan from Pennsylvania and Somers Point, so I am grateful for your—and Deputy Gorelick, thank you again. As an alumnus of the Justice Department, I appreciate the service of both of you and continuing to follow this 10 years later.

I just want to attach myself for a minute for the record, but I think your supporting the concept of what my friend, the gentleman, Mr. Barber, just explored, I note your report calls it the most important unfulfilled recommendation of the 9/11 Commission is the Congressional oversight issue that was just identified. I think we need to take it to heart. The fragmented oversight is an impediment to the Department's successful development, but it has also made Americans less safe.

This is a critically important thing. I thank you for your testimony. I am not going to ask you to expound on it further, but I hope we can take your testimony and invoke the importance of that with my colleagues to revisit this issue.

In the moments that I do have, one of the issues that you also both identified in the report is the emerging threat, which wasn't at the heart of 9/11, and it is the cyber domain and the recognition that our policies are not keeping pace with the breathtaking, rapid advances in technology.

You look for a number of things to be done. Perhaps you can tell me in your words what you think the most important things we ought to be doing and how we ought to be doing a better job communicating with citizens out there about the nature of the threat, what they can do to help us make ourselves more secure from what could be a remarkably devastating impact of a cyber attack.

Mr. KEAN. Jamie has talked about this, I think very articulately, but it is a silent threat as far as most of the public is concerned. They just don't see it. I mean, somebody says, well, we lost some information that the Department of Defense had to a cyber attack. Somebody got some information. Or this Boeing was doing a new invention of some sort or a new technology, and somebody in China got it, and you sort of read that in the newspaper and you read something else.

But it is not real to people, because it is quiet. Partly because Government—neither Government nor the private sector likes to admit they have had things stolen and they don't have them anymore. So the public is not as aware as it ought to be of the cyber threat and why it is important.

I think Jamie hit it right when she said, you know, getting the Government to combine with the private sector, most of the infrastructure is in the private sector. It is not in the Government. We have to protect the Government, obviously, but we have also got to protect the private sector, because it is not only technological future, but it is our economic future. If we allow the innovation that this country has always been known for to be stolen from us, we are allowing this country to undergo great harm.

So I think when Jamie says getting the Government to really work with the private sector and help the private sector and get the private sector to trust Government so their expertise can be put together to protect not just the Government, but also the private sector, is absolutely what should be done.

Ms. GORELICK. There is a woodenness in the interaction between the private sector and the Government on this issue that is not optimal. There is a—there are real inhibitions to the private sector sharing a vulnerability with the Government. There are liabilities that attach. There are huge inhibitions to the Government protecting not just its own computers, but the privately-held computers on which our security rests. These are tough, tough issues because we are not used to having our military operate domestically, which is really underlying this entire debate.

The resources to help the private sector fight back rest in our military. We don't usually deploy our military to help a domestic entity defend itself. That is at the crux of the problem. These are tough issues.

I would try to get underneath them to understand them, to see if we are matching up what we ask of our Government with what the threat is, because one of the things we said in our original report was that the most—one of the most natural things to do is to define away the hard part of your job. NORAD gave to the FAA the hard part of its job. NORAD said, our Defense Department said we will take care of the threat up until the U.S. border. You take care of the threat inside the United States.

So nobody with any actual force and power, because the FAA doesn't have an Air Force, had the job of thinking about and preparing for and addressing someone hijacking a plane domestically. So it was a gap. If you had said to our Defense Department, "We want you to defend the United States not only against a plane coming across from Russia, but somebody hijacking a plane in the United States," we would have had a robust plan. We had no such plan.

I think we are in the equivalent place today, where we are so worried about using our military capabilities in aid of a domestic vulnerability that we are not doing what we need to do. We are putting our heads in the sand. I think we heard that from pretty much every member of the National security community with whom we spoke.

Mr. MEEHAN. Where do you go? Where do you go with authorizing private companies to take some action on their own that would be responsive what are cyber intrusions into their own databases?

Ms. GORELICK. Congressman Meehan, that is a very good question. So if I own an ISP or I own a telephone company today and

I am attacked, I am probably experiencing that attack through two other private systems. Can I go through those private systems to counterattack? No. I am disabled. That is a really important problem, an inhibition to keeping us safer.

I think there are hard issues, to be sure. There are hard issues. But having no solution is not the right solution.

Mr. MEEHAN. Well, I thank you for your testimony on this. I think we could spend an entire hearing focused on that issue and others. I think that it is important that you do know, consistent with this report, and your recommendations, we have gotten out of the full committee in a bipartisan fashion very substantive cyber legislation that we hope may actually get onto the floor in the coming weeks that begins to create the relationship, working with FBI, NSA, and others, putting the DHS as the civilian interface with the private sector, working on issues of liability that would enhance the willingness and readiness to collaborate and communicate in a timely manner on the threats that they are facing, because as the Governor said, 90 percent of the assets are in private hands.

It is a different situation than we have ever faced before. We think this is an important next step, but only a next step on what needs to be a continuing emphasis. Thank you for your great work and your very important testimony that helps us create a record that allows us to continue to move from this to the kind of constructive reform and expansion of the responsibilities that we have got to deal with on here. Thank you so much for your service.

Chairman MCCAUL. Let me thank you for your leadership on the cybersecurity bill that hopefully will get passed next week on the floor.

Let me thank the two of you, Governor and Ms. Gorelick, for your service, and all members of the 9/11 Commission for your great work on this report and service to the American people to protect them. I think Congress could be doing a better job in reorganizing itself to protect the American people, rather than squabble over jurisdictional lines. I think every Member of Congress is responsible if something does happen, will be responsible if we don't fix this problem.

Ultimately, while Chairmen will fight and never give up jurisdiction, I have found as a Chairman, it is really up to leadership to make that call. It is up to our leadership to step forward and take responsibility to do what is right for the American people.

So, again, thank you for being here today. With that, this committee stands adjourned.

[Whereupon, at 11:50 a.m., the committee was adjourned.]

○

www.ingramcontent.com/pod-product-compliance
Lightning Source LLC
Chambersburg PA
CBHW080631290526
45790CB00007B/3012